EMERGENCY 999!
FIRE SERVICE

Kathryn Walker
Photography by Chris Fairclough

Published in 2013 by Wayland

Copyright © Wayland 2013

Wayland
338 Euston Road
London NW1 3BH

Wayland Australia
Level 17/207 Kent Street
Sydney, NSW 2000

Produced for Wayland by Discovery Books Ltd
Wayland series editor: Katie Powell
Editor: James Nixon
Designer: Ian Winton
Commissioned photography: Chris Fairclough

The author, publisher and Discovery Books Ltd would like to thank
South Wales Fire and Rescue Service for their help and participation in this book.

Picture credits: Shutterstock: pp. 4 top (Harald Hoiland Tjostheim), 6 bottom (Margot
Petrowski), 12 middle (Monkey Business Images), 13 top, 20 top (Tatiana Belova), 23 bottom
(Monkey Business Images); South Wales Fire and Rescue Service: pp. 7, 11 bottom, 17
top, 21 bottom, 25 top, 26 bottom, 30; West Midlands Fire Service Photographic 2010: pp. 4
bottom, 5, 6 top, 11 top, 13 bottom, 15 bottom, 16, 17 bottom, 18, 19, 20 bottom, 21 top, 22 top,
26 top, 27, 28, 29 top, 31.

British Library Cataloguing in Publication Data
Walker, Kathryn, 1957-
   Fire service. -- (Emergency 999)
   1. Fire departments--Juvenile literature. 2. Fire
fighters--Juvenile literature.
   I. Title II. Series
   363.3'78-dc22
   ISBN: 978 0 7502 7883 6

Printed in China
10 9 8 7 6 5 4 3 2 1

Wayland is a division of Hachette Children's Books,
an Hachette UK company. www.hachette.co.uk

Note to parents and teachers: Every effort has been made by the Publishers to ensure that
the websites in this book are suitable for children, that they are of the highest educational
value, and that they contain no inappropriate or offensive material. However, because of the
nature of the Internet, it is impossible to guarantee that the contents of these sites will not be
altered. We strongly advise that Internet access is supervised by a responsible adult.

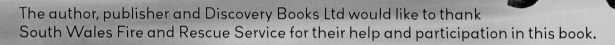

CONTENTS

CALL THE FIRE BRIGADE!

Fire can be deadly. A fire that breaks out in a building, or an outdoor fire that gets out of control must be reported quickly. We need to telephone 999 and ask for the fire service. We can also dial 112 – a number for the emergency services that is used in most European countries.

Smoke, fumes and flames can be deadly. Firefighters must be well-protected when tackling a blaze.

999 Notes

Small fires can quickly become big fires that can kill. No matter how small the fire is, phone 999 or 112 and ask for the fire service. Emergency calls are free, even from mobile phones.

Not just fire

Fires are not the only type of emergency that the Fire and Rescue Service deal with. Firefighters are called out to floods, **chemical spills** and to rescue people from collapsed buildings or car crashes. They are often called to rescue animals, too.

An important part of a firefighter's work is helping to free people from vehicles that have been involved in road accidents.

Putting you through

When you phone 999, your call is answered by a telephone operator. He or she will ask you which emergency service you require. If it is the fire service, the operator puts you through to a Fire and Rescue Control Centre.

A Fire and Rescue Control Centre deals with emergency calls over a large area of the country.

FIRE CONTROL CENTRE

When your call is put through to the Fire and Rescue Control Centre, the operator there will ask you what the emergency is and if anyone is trapped or hurt.

When answering a 999 call, operators use computer systems to find the nearest available fire engines.

Where are you?

You will need to tell the operator where the emergency is. If you are in the open countryside or not sure of the exact address, look for nearby **landmarks**. If you are reporting an incident on a road or motorway, try to give the road number and name of the nearest town or village.

Knowing how to help

The operator keys all the details you give into a computer and decides how many fire engines – also called **appliances** – to send. The operator is also trained to give life-saving advice to a caller who may be in danger.

FACE-TO-FACE

Denise – Fire Control Operator

I work day and night **shifts**, as part of a team or **watch**. We get calls about all types of incidents – from people trapped in burning buildings to cows stuck in mud. I send out help and stay in touch with the crews by radio until their work is finished.

Sometimes I have to tell callers what to do to stay safe. When people are very scared or in danger, I keep talking to them until help arrives. One of the best things about this job is being able to help people.

GETTING THERE FAST

When the operator keys your information into the computer system, the screen immediately shows which appliances are closest to the emergency. This system turns on the alarms at the nearest fire station.

All systems go!

The address and details of the emergency are sent through to a machine called a teleprinter (right) and the firefighters rush to their appliances.

Quick getaway

Firefighters then have to put on special protective clothing called a fire kit. Firefighters keep their kit ready by the appliance so they can put it on as fast a possible.

Firefighters quickly put on their fire kit before setting off to answer a call.

The appliance rushes off with lights flashing and sirens sounding. This warns motorists to pull over and let the firefighters through. In an emergency, every second counts.

999 Notes

If you call 999 to report an incident on a motorway or road, call from one of the SOS phones at the roadside if possible. That way the operator will know exactly where you are calling from. This could save precious time.

DRESSED FOR ACTION

When firefighters are in the fire station, they wear a uniform of comfortable trousers, tee shirts and shirts. But on a call-out they need clothes that will protect them from heat, flames and falling objects. This fire kit goes on over the station uniform.

Here is the basic fire kit:

torch

radio

plastic visor protects the face

hard plastic helmet protects the head from falling objects. Hood worn under the helmet protects the neck, ears and hair from heat and fire

thick gloves protect the hands from fire, heat and sharp objects

jacket and trousers made of strong material protect from the heat and flames

strong, rubber boots with thick soles and metal toe caps to protect the feet

An officer keeps a record of how long firefighters have been in a smoke-filled building on a whiteboard.

Getting air

When firefighters go into a place where there is smoke or dangerous gas, they wear breathing apparatus so they can breathe safely. This breathing apparatus has a long, narrow container filled with air, called an **air cylinder**. It is strapped to the firefighter's back and connected by a tube to a face mask.

999 Notes

Distress Signal Units (DSUs) are devices that are clipped on to breathing apparatus. When a firefighter gets into difficulty, he or she uses the DSU to sound an alarm. If the firefighter is injured and stops moving, the DSU automatically sends a signal for help.

air cylinder

DSU

face mask

The fire service use different types of appliances. A 'rescue pump' is the most common type. It carries a water tank, pumping equipment, ladders, hoses and rescue tools. A rescue pump may be sent out to deal with house fires or road accidents.

water tank

A hose is attached to the pump and water supply at the back of the fire appliance.

hose

Extra help

A rescue pump also has equipment for freeing people from crashed cars and other small spaces. This includes special tools for cutting through metal or glass and moving wreckage.

Firefighters unload the cutting tools that they need to get someone out of a crashed car.

A firefighter begins to cut his way through a smashed car so the driver can be freed safely.

Reaching high

Aerial ladder platforms (ALPs) may be sent to fires in high buildings. This vehicle carries an extending ladder that reaches higher than the ladders on rescue pumps. It can also reach downwards, below the ground. There is a cage at the end of the ladder. Firefighters can stand in this cage to spray water on to a fire or to rescue people.

cage

999 Notes

Not all appliances carry ladders and hoses. At an incident where several fire engines are sent out, an Incident Command Unit (ICU) may also be used. An ICU is like a mobile office where fire officers plan and control an operation using computers, phones, maps and radios.

FIGHTING FIRE

When a rescue pump is called out to a fire, it has a team of four or five firefighters on board. One drives and two put on breathing apparatus to go into the fire area. A watch manager leads the team and is responsible for their safety.

FACE-TO-FACE

Jeff – Watch Manager

I work two day shifts, two long night shifts and then I have four days off. Like all firefighters, I spend a lot of my shift training, checking equipment and advising people on how to prevent fires.

When we are called out, I'm in charge of the crew on my appliance. I try to make sure they stay safe. Afterwards, I fill out a report about the incident and look for ways to improve what we do.

Getting water

All rescue pumps carry a tank of water, but when there is a big blaze, firefighters look for a **fire hydrant**. This is a point in the ground where they can attach hoses to draw water from the local water supply. If there is a water shortage in the area, a water carrier is sent out. This is a vehicle that carries thousands of litres of water.

Clearing up

After putting out the fire, firefighters clean up as much as they can. Back at the station, they discuss what happened and clean the appliances ready for the next call-out.

fire hydrant

Firefighters' duties include cleaning their equipment after a call-out and at the end of a shift.

ROPE RESCUE

People or animals sometimes need rescuing from places that are hard to reach. They might be injured on a mountainside, trapped down a shaft or **stranded** in a river. The Fire and Rescue Service have special teams called rope rescue units to deal with these situations.

harness

Rope rescue units are skilled in using ropes to reach and move people or animals to safety. They use harnesses, slings and **stretchers** together with devices for attaching and pulling on the ropes.

Using ropes, an injured person on a cliff side can be hauled to safety on a stretcher.

Rope rescue skills help keep firefighters safe when they work on high buildings.

Rope practice

The teams practise their skills on cliff sides, in **gorges** (right) or even at the fire station. Sometimes they take part in rope rescue competitions, where a rescue scene is set up with dummies instead of real people. Teams from around the country compete to see who can carry out the rescue in the quickest and safest way.

999 Notes

Firefighters are sometimes called to rescue animals. This could be anything from horses stuck in ditches to cats trapped down drains. Trying to rescue animals can be very dangerous for both the rescuer and the animal. Rescue teams have to study how to handle different types of animals in difficult situations.

Firefighters use slings to pull a horse to safety. Great care is needed to avoid causing the animal distress.

WATER RESCUE

When people or animals get into trouble in the water, the Fire and Rescue Service are often called to help. They go to emergencies in or near waterways, such as rivers, lakes and canals. They also help when there are floods.

Teams of firefighters are trained to deal with incidents that involve fast-moving water, still water, ice or mud. These are the water rescue units.

When there is serious flooding, firefighters are called out to rescue people stranded in their cars.

Rescue vehicles

Water rescue units use **off-road** vehicles that are packed with equipment such as ropes and rescue **dinghies**. The vehicles may also be used to tow rescue boats to the emergency.

Firefighters use small boats to rescue people who have become stranded by floodwater.

Floating aids

Other water rescue equipment includes **life jackets** and ice paths. An ice path is quickly inflated to make a floating platform for rescuing people trapped in ice, mud or water.

life jacket

ice path

Inflatable hoses can be used as rescue lines or stretched across fast-moving water to stop people being swept away.

throw line

This rescue line called a 'throw line' is used to pull a person to safety from the water's edge.

999 Notes

Don't try to walk through floodwater – just 15 centimetres of fast-moving water can knock you off your feet. There may also be dangers underneath the floodwater that you cannot see. The water may have lifted manhole covers and swept them away, leaving deep and deadly holes.

Urban Search and Rescue (USAR) units are teams of firefighters trained to deal with emergencies where people are trapped in collapsed structures. The teams also rescue people stuck in small spaces or other difficult places.

USAR firefighters are skilled in clearing wreckage and making areas safe.

sniffer dog

USAR teams sometimes use sniffer dogs to help them locate survivors buried beneath the rubble of collapsed buildings.

Dealing with disaster

If a major disaster such as a rail crash or an explosion happens, USAR teams from across the UK work together. Major USAR incidents can be caused by natural events such as storms or hurricanes. They may also be caused by bombs.

999 Notes

To find trapped people USAR teams use special equipment, such as listening devices that pick up faint sounds, and cameras that reach deep into the wreckage.

camera

Rescuers use cameras on poles that they push into gaps in the rubble to help them find trapped people.

Dangerous materials

Sometimes accidents cause dangerous materials to be released. A road crash could result in a chemical spill that is a danger to people and animals. Fire engines carry some equipment to deal with small spills, but for bigger ones there are teams called Environmental Protection Units (EPUs).

EPUs carry special pumps for removing dangerous substances and materials that can soak them up.

CAUTION VEHICLES

T16

When dealing with spills of dangerous chemicals, EPUs wear protective clothing that completely covers their bodies.

AT THE FIRE STATION

Fire stations have to answer an emergency call at any time of day or night. Small stations are often crewed by **retained firefighters** – men and women who may have other jobs but can be called to an emergency. Larger stations are staffed by firefighters who work full shifts. These are called **wholetime firefighters**.

Starting a shift

Each shift starts with a parade to check everyone is present. Then the watch manager tells everyone on his or her team which appliance they will be riding on and what their duties will be.

Firefighters line up for their watch parade.

Fit for action

A fire station has sleeping quarters and a canteen (right). Firefighters use up lots of energy while on a shift, so eating well is important.

Firefighters also need to stay very fit, so some stations have a gym.

FACE-TO-FACE

Derek – Wholetime Firefighter

After the watch parade, the first job is to check the equipment and appliances. When we are not out answering a call, we do lots of training and practice. We also visit homes to fit smoke alarms or chat about fire safety. At the end of the shift, we hose down the appliances.

Teamwork is extremely important because we need to trust and support each other. Sometimes, we see things that upset us, but it feels great to be able to save lives.

PRACTICE, PRACTICE!

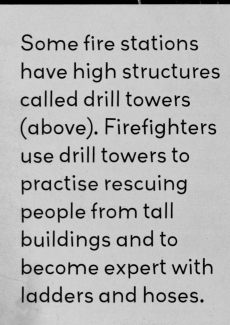

To be prepared for any emergency, firefighters need lots of practice. They need to practise what to do in different types of situations and learn how to use new equipment.

Training yard

Behind a fire station, there is a **drill yard** where crews practise and train. Sometimes old scrapyard cars are brought there so that firefighters can practise using cutting equipment.

Some fire stations have high structures called drill towers (above). Firefighters use drill towers to practise rescuing people from tall buildings and to become expert with ladders and hoses.

They also train in buildings called 'smoke houses'. These are filled with smoke so that firefighters can practise using breathing apparatus and finding their way through a dark building.

Training exercises in a smoke house allow firefighters to experience the difficulties of working inside a smoke-filled building.

Getting familiar

Firefighters need a good knowledge of their local area. They get to know the larger buildings and where the water hydrants are. Then, if a fire breaks out, firefighters won't waste time trying to find their way about.

999 Notes

A smoke house gives firefighters a chance to practise using a piece of equipment called the **thermal imaging camera**. This uses the heat that objects or people give off, and turns them into images. Firefighters use these cameras to find people in heavy smoke or darkness.

This firefighter tests a thermal imaging camera. It detects body heat and shows it on the camera screen.

FIRE SAFETY

Fire prevention is an important part of a firefighter's job. One of the ways firefighters help prevent fires is through home fire-safety checks.

Anyone who wants their home checked can contact their local fire station to arrange a visit.

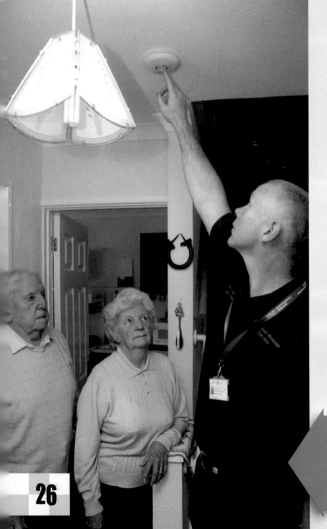

Looking for danger

When firefighters visit, they look for anything that could be a fire risk. This could be electrical wires worn through or **sockets** with too many plugs in them. Firefighters point out what the fire hazards are and explain how to make things safe.

Firefighters will also fit smoke alarms. The loud bleeping of these alarms has saved many lives. It is important to check them regularly – an alarm with a dead battery is useless!

During a home fire-safety check, a firefighter checks that a smoke alarm is working properly.

999 Notes

Every household should make a fire escape plan:

- First, choose an escape route – the best one is usually the normal way you leave your home
- Choose a second route in case the normal way out is blocked by fire
- Decide on a safe place to meet up outside the home
- Decide on a place you can all go to if you can't escape. This should be a room with a window and where you can use a phone
- Make sure everyone knows where keys to doors and windows are kept
- Practise the plan together.

This boy is learning about fire hazards at a Fire Safety Centre. Can you spot anything here that would cause a fire?

SPREADING THE WORD

Firefighters work hard to make sure adults and children understand the dangers of fire and how to prevent it. They visit local schools to give talks on fire safety and explain what to do if a fire breaks out.

Jokes that can kill

Firefighters also discuss the problems of **arson** and **hoax** calls. Arson is when someone deliberately starts a fire. Hoax calls are when people call 999 and pretend there is an emergency. Like arson, making a hoax call is a crime. It can cost lives by preventing firefighters going to real emergencies.

A class of schoolchildren are taught the dangers of fire at the Fire Safety Centre.

Open days

Fire stations hold open days, where families can visit and firefighters demonstrate their rescue skills. These events encourage people to think about working for the Fire and Rescue Service.

A firefighter hands out leaflets about the Fire and Rescue Service in a shopping centre.

FACE-TO-FACE

Andy – Retained Firefighter

I work in an office near my home, but I am also a retained firefighter. This means that when my **alerter** bleeps (left), I have to stop whatever I am doing. I have five minutes to get to my local fire station for a call-out.

I may get called out three or four times a week, but this varies. Once a week we have a practice night at the station, when we test equipment and train. I enjoy being a part-time firefighter because I like doing two very different jobs.

DO YOU HAVE WHAT IT TAKES?

If you want to become a firefighter, you need to work hard and do well at school. When you are 18 years old, you can apply for a job as a firefighter. Then you will take some written tests, fitness tests and have a medical examination to see if you are a suitable candidate.

If all the tests go well, you will spend some months at a firefighters' training school. After that, you can begin work at a fire station, training and learning all the time while you work as a firefighter.

Could you be a firefighter?

Look at the following questions and answer 'yes' or 'no'.

- Are you interested in helping all kinds of people?

- Do you like working as part of a team?

- Are you someone who always turns up for appointments on time and doesn't let other people down?

- Are you willing to take orders and follow strict rules?

- Would you be willing to work long days and nights, sometimes when other people are on holiday?

- Can you stay calm and think clearly in difficult situations?

- Are you willing to work hard at keeping fit and strong?

- Are you interested in saving lives and in helping people to stay safe in their homes?

If you answered 'yes' to all these questions, then maybe you do have what it takes to be a firefighter.

GLOSSARY

air cylinder the part of a breathing apparatus set in which air is stored

alerter a small device that bleeps or vibrates to let you know that someone wishes to contact you

appliance fire engine or other vehicle used by the Fire and Rescue Service

arson deliberately starting a fire

chemical spill an accident where chemicals have been released

dinghy small, inflatable rubber boat

drill yard an area at the back of a fire station where crews practise and train

fire hydrant a pipe in a street from which firefighters can draw water

gorge a narrow valley with steep, rocky sides

hoax a trick or joke to fool people into believing something is true

landmark an object or building that can be easily noticed or recognised

life jacket an inflatable jacket without sleeves for keeping a person afloat in water

off-road describes something that is designed to be used away from public roads and across rough land

rescue pump the most common type of fire engine that carries basic firefighting equipment

retained firefighter someone who works part-time as a firefighter and who may also have a full-time job

shift the period of hours that a group of people work

socket an electrical device with slots into which a plug is fitted

stranded left in a helpless position, without a way to escape

stretcher a device for carrying sick or injured people

thermal imaging camera a camera that forms an image from heat given off by objects. It can show an image of a person in the dark because the body gives off heat

watch the team of firefighters or call operators who are on duty together for a fixed time or shift

wholetime firefighter someone who has a full-time job as a firefighter

INDEX AND FURTHER INFORMATION

Websites

These pages on the Hampshire Fire and Rescue Service website have lots of information and activities about fire safety for all age groups:
http://www.hantsfire.gov.uk/kidzone.htm

The London Fire Brigade have games and activities that will teach you how to keep safe from fire. Go to: **http://www.london-fire.gov.uk/GamesAndActivities.asp**

To find out about what firefighters do and lots about fire safety, try this website:
http://kids.direct.gov.uk/main.aspx?firstObject=fire_station

Books

Helping Hands: At the Fire Station, Ruth Thomson, Wayland 2008
In Time of Need: Fire, Sean Connolly, Franklin Watts, 2004